Published by:

Rosh Review, LLC

P.O. Box 7021

Huntington Woods, MI 48070

D1738863

This book is designed to provide information and guidance in regard to the subject matter concerned. It is to be used as a study guide for preparing for classroom exams and certification exams. It is not meant to be a clinical manual. The reader is advised to consult textbooks and other reference manuals in making clinical decisions. It is not the purpose of this book to reprint all the information that is otherwise available, but rather to assist the student in organizing the material to facilitate study and recall on exams. Although every precaution has been taken in the preparation of this book, the publisher, author, and members of the editorial board assume no responsibility for errors, omissions or typographical mistakes. Nor is any liability assumed for damages resulting from the direct and indirect use of the information contained herein. To the best of our knowledge, the book contains information that is up-to-date up to the printing date. Due to the very nature of the medical profession, there will be points out-of-date as soon as the book is available to you. If you do not wish to be bound by the above, you may return this book for a full refund if a monetary cost was incurred in obtaining the book.

Rosh RAPID REVIEW
for the PANCE / PANRE
1st Edition

Dermatologic System

Yehuda Wolf, PA-C

Emily Oslie, PA-C

Adam Rosh, MD

Your Content Creation Team

Yehuda Wolf, PA-C

Yehuda joined the Rosh team in 2015 while still a student in PA school. As Rapid Review author and editor-in-chief, Yehuda continues to ensure the Rapid Reviews are of the highest caliber and standards. Yehuda graduated from Touro College New York with a Masters in Physician Assistant Studies with Honors. Yehuda currently spends his time between a busy pediatric primary care practice and pediatric surgical urology.

Emily Oslie, PA-C

Emily Oslie graduated with a B.S. in applied human biology from Seattle Pacific University where she played volleyball competitively. After graduation, she worked as a medical scribe in emergency departments and a primary care office in Seattle while applying to PA programs. Emily attended the Duke Physician Assistant Program where she served as class president and earned her PA certification and masters in health sciences. She is currently working at Duke Urgent Care in Durham, North Carolina.

Adam Rosh, MD

Dr. Adam Rosh is the founder of Rosh Review, which he created in 2011. He received his B.A. in biochemistry and M.S. in microbiology from the University of Wisconsin, Madison. He received his medical degree from Rutgers Medical School and completed his emergency medicine residency training at New York University/Bellevue Hospital Center, where he was chief resident. Dr. Rosh went on to serve as assistant residency director and residency director at Detroit Receiving Hospital. He is the author and editor of Pretest Emergency Medicine and Case Files Emergency Medicine both published by McGraw Hill. He currently is the CEO of Rosh Review and an Attending Emergency Physician.

Your Content Support Team

Kristian Savic, Copy Editor

Kristian is Senior Content Editor at Rosh Review. Originally hailing from Salzburg, Austria, his training includes three years in med school, a B.S. in communication sciences, and an M.A. in German literature–all of which helped in creating the passionate stickler for format, grammar, and bio-science terminology he is today. Kristian's work is focused on making sure Rosh Review content is well written, correct, and adhering to our house style and good science writing standards.

Erica Parrish, Content Manager

Erica Parrish received her B.A. in biology from the College of St. Scholastica and her D.C. from Northwestern Health Sciences University. She gained clinical experience serving patients in both Minnesota and Florida before joining the team at Rosh Review.

All Of You, Content Impactors

Although most of the content in this book was created by our author team, over the years we've received so much input from our subscribers, we want to shine a light on this contribution. Every comment or feedback email we receive is reviewed, discussed, and if agreed upon, implemented. The power of all of you, contributing your experience and insights, allows us to continually improve the quality of the content we publish. This process is perpetual. As medicine changes, our content must change with it. We value the content partnership we have and hope you'll continue to raise expectations.

Shout Outs

Yehuda Wolf, PA-C

I am still in shell shock. This project has been years in the making and the original reason why I ever reached out to Adam. I can't believe we are finally done. First, I need to thank my most amazing wife and children for their unparalleled support and encouragement. Thank you for allowing me to do work after I finally got home from work. A special thank you to my mentors Dr. Hylton Lightman, MD and Dov Landa, PA-C whose mentorship and guidance continually make me a better provider to my patients. Thanks to my right-hand Emily and the rest of the team, Kristian and Erica. You are truly the ink to my pen, the paper to my pad and without you this project would be nothing but a sloppy mess in my mind. Thank you Adam for your constant support and encouragement. Always pushing us "one step further." Finally, I would like to thank the One Above for His Goodness and His Grace that He has shown me throughout my life. May this be the first of many more projects to come. In the words of the ancient physician Maimonides, "Never allow the thought to arise in me that I have attained to sufficient knowledge, but vouchsafe to me the strength, the leisure and the ambition ever to extend my knowledge. For art is great, but the mind of man is ever expanding."

Emily Oslie, PA-C

This is is for my parents, Myron and Sherri, who have cheered me on through each phase of my education and career; my sister, Maddie; my classmates at Duke who supported me and are the reason I have countless fond memories of my time in the program; the instructors, advisors, and clinical preceptors who challenged me to become a compassionate and competent provider; my co-providers, mentor, supervising physician, and patients at Duke Urgent Care who make me a better PA every day.

Adam Rosh, MD

A hearty thanks goes out to my family for their love and support, Danielle, Ruby, Rhys, and especially my parents, Karl and Marcia; the incredibly dedicated team at Rosh Review who relentlessly raise expectations; the committed medical professionals of Rutgers Medical School, the emergency medicine departments at New York University/Bellevue Hospital Center, and Wayne State University/Detroit Receiving Hospital; and my patients, who put their trust in me, and teach me something new each day.

Purpose & Goals of this Book

Learning and education is a dynamic process, one that is never ending. Once we commit to a life in medicine, we commit to a life of learning. The Rosh Rapid Review book series is best suited to serve as an adjunct to your medical education. It is not meant as a primary source, rather it should help you organize your thoughts and provide ancillary knowledge for a more robust education. We are counting on you to not just regurgitate facts, but rather, paraphrasing Dr. Elizabeth Blackburn, to learn how it all works. We are privileged to be in the role of caretaker and thus have a responsibility to our patients to be the most knowledgeable we can be. Use this book on your learning journey. At some point, you will grow out of it. But in the meantime, we hope the hard work by the dedicated Rosh Review team can play just a small role in helping you reach your goals and achieve your dreams.

Adam Rosh, MD
Founder, Rosh Review

"To study the phenomena of disease without books is to sail an uncharted sea, while to study books without patients is not to go to sea at all."

William Osler, Aequanimatas

"I didn't want to just know the names of things. I remember really wanting to know how it all worked."

Elizabeth Blackburn,
Nobel Prize for Physiology or Medicine

Rosh ✓ Core Values

1. We pay attention to detail and always deliver the highest quality content.

2. We believe it is a privilege to interact with and care for individuals.

3. We are always learning and continuously self improving, it is part of our DNA.

Even after multiple reviews, there is sure to be mistakes in this book. As part of Rosh Review's culture of continuously learning, please let us know if you identify an error by sending us an email to alwaysimproving@roshreview.com

Let's get started...

Dermatologic System

DERMATOLOGIC SYSTEM
Table of Contents

I. Acneiform Eruptions

ACNE VULGARIS • FOLLICULITIS • ROSACEA

A. Acne Vulgaris

Pathophysiology
- **Most commonly** caused by **Propionibacterium acnes** (formerly known as **Propionibacterium acnes**)

Patient
- Adolescent

Presentation
- Rash on face, neck, upper chest, back

Physical Exam
- Closed comedones (**whiteheads**), open comedones (**blackheads**), papules, and pustules

Management
- Mild to moderate: topical retinoids, topical antibiotics, or benzoyl peroxide
- Moderate to severe: add oral antibiotics
- Severe: oral isotretinoin (**Pregnancy class X, must have two methods of birth control**)

Comedonal (noninflammatory) acne
- **Topical retinoid**
- **Azelaic acid/salicylic acid** (alts)

Mild papulopustular and mixed acne
- **Topical antimicrobial (benzoyl peroxide/ antibiotic) AND**
- **Topical retinoid**
  OR
- **Benzoyl peroxide & topical antibiotic**

Moderate papulopustular and mixed acne
- **Topical retinoid** AND
- **Oral antibiotic** AND
- **Topical benzoyl peroxide**

Severe acne
- **Topical retinoid** AND
- **Oral antibiotic** AND
- **Topical benzoyl peroxide**
  OR
- **Oral isotretinoin monotherapy**

B. Folliculitis

Pathophysiology
- **Most commonly** caused by **S. aureus**
- If recent **hot tub use** – **Pseudomonas**

Presentation
- Dome-shaped pustules with erythematous halos
- Hair follicle at the **center** of each lesion

Management
- Topical: **mupirocin**
- Oral: oxacillin, dicloxacillin, and cefuroxime
- Ciprofloxacin (for "hot tub" folliculitis)

C. Rosacea

Presentation
- **Acne-like rash** on the **forehead, cheeks and nose** that gets worse with ingestion of **alcohol, hot drinks** and **spicy foods**

Physical Exam
- Facial flushing, **telangiectasias**, skin coarsening, **rhinophyma** (bulbous nose), and **absence of comedones**

Management
- Topical **metronidazole**

Triggers for flushing
- Extremes of temperature
- Sunlight
- Spicy foods
- Alcohol
- Exercise
- Acute psychological stressors
- Medications
- Menopausal hot flashes

Epidomology
- More common in lightly pigmented skin
- Adults older than 30 years of age (can occur in adolescents)
- Women > Men

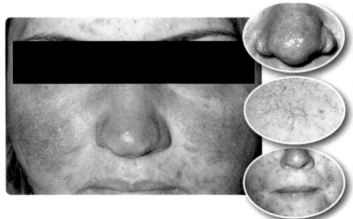

Phymatous changes (rhinophyma)
Tissue hypertrophy, irregular contours

Telangiectasia
Visible, enlarged cutaneous blood vessels

Papules and pustules
Central face, may be mistaken for acne

II. Desquamation

ERYTHEMA MULTIFORME • STEVENS-JOHNSON SYNDROME • TOXIC EPIDERMAL NECROLYSIS

A. Erythema Multiforme (EM)

Pathophysiology
- **Most commonly** caused by **herpes simplex virus (HSV)**

Presentation
- **Acute onset** of symmetric target lesions on palms and soles; face and trunk may also be involved

Physical Exam
- **Target-like** lesions with a **central dark papule** surrounded by a **pale area** and a **"halo"** of erythema

Management
- Supportive care; lesions are usually self-limiting

Causes
- Herpes simplex (most common viral cause)
- Mycoplasma
- Sulfonamides
- Penicillins
- Barbiturates
- Phenytoin
- Lupus
- Hepatitis
- Lymphoma

Comments
- Common drugs that cause EM: **S**ulfa, **O**ral hypoglycemics, **A**nticonvulsants, **P**enicillin, NSAIDs (**SOAPS**)

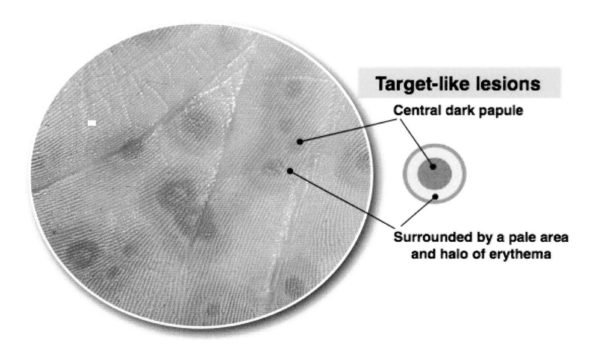

Target-like lesions

Central dark papule

Surrounded by a pale area and halo of erythema

B. Stevens-Johnson Syndrome

Pathophysiology
- **Most commonly** caused by a reaction to medications

Physical Exam
- Vesicles and bullae **involving < 10% of the body surface area including mucous membranes**

Management
- Referral to **burn center**

Comments
- **SCORTEN** score is used to determine the prognosis and clinical setting for treatment

C. Toxic Epidermal Necrolysis

Patient
- Elderly, increased risk if HIV positive

Physical Exam
- Vesicles and bullae **involving > 30% of the body surface area including mucous membranes**

- **Positive Nikolsky** sign (extension of lesion with lateral pressure)

Management
- Referral to **burn center**

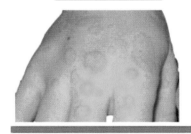

Erythema multiforme

Stevens-Johnson syndrome

Toxic epidermal necrolysis

- < 10% TBSA
- Most common on hands/forearms
- Target lesions
- Oral lesions (50%)

- < 10% TBSA
- Most common in children
- URI-like prodrome
- Most due to drug reactions
- ≥ 2 mucosal sites
- Admit to burn center

- > 30% TBSA
- Most common in elderly
- HIV individuals with increased
- Abrupt onset
- Positive Nikolsky sign
- Mucous membrane involveme
- Admit to burn center

III. Diseases / Disorders of the Hair and Nails

ALOPECIA • ONYCHOMYCOSIS • PARONYCHIA

A. Alopecia

Pathophysiology
- **Traction Alopecia**: caused primarily by pulling force being applied to the hair (tight hairstyles)
- **Telogen Effluvium**: diffuse hair loss that occurs after stress, illness, medication
- **Androgenetic Alopecia**: typical male pattern baldness

B. Alopecia Areata

Pathophysiology
- **Most common** cause is **autoimmune**

Patient
- History of other autoimmune disorder

Physical Exam
- Patches of **smooth**, **non-scarring hair loss** with patches
  of smaller hairs termed "**exclamation hairs**"

Management
- Intralesional corticosteroids

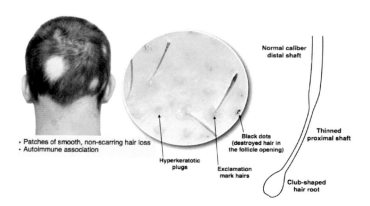

- Patches of smooth, non-scarring hair loss
- Autoimmune association

Normal caliber distal shaft
Black dots (destroyed hair in the follicle opening)
Hyperkeratotic plugs
Exclamation mark hairs
Thinned proximal shaft
Club-shaped hair root

C. Androgenetic Alopecia

(Male pattern hair loss)

Most common type of hair loss in men

Loss of terminal hairs in characteristic distribution

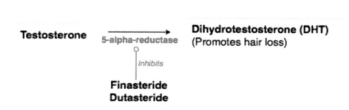

Testosterone →(5-alpha-reductase)→ Dihydrotestosterone (DHT) (Promotes hair loss)

Inhibits

Finasteride
Dutasteride

Management
- Surgery (e.g. follicular unit transplant)
- 5-alpha-reductase inhibitors (e.g. finasteride)
- Laser therapy
- Platelet-rich plasma

D. Onychomycosis

Physical Exam
- Thickened and discolored toenails

Diagnostic Studies
- **KOH** preparation of nail scrapings

Management
- **Oral terbinafine**

Comments
- Serum aminotransferases should be monitored before starting treatment with terbinafine and during the treatment due to **hepatotoxicity**

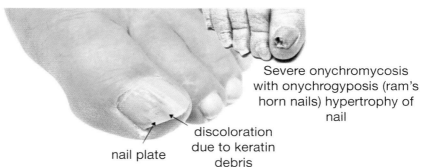

Severe onychromycosis with onychrogyposis (ram's horn nails) hypertrophy of nail

discoloration due to keratin debris

nail plate

Oral Antifungal Agents for the Treatment of Onychomycosis			
Terbinafine	First-line	250 mg daily x 12 wks	Yes; liver enzymes
Itraconazole	Alternative first-line	200 mg daily x 12 wks	Yes; liver enzymes
Fluconazole	Not FDA approved	150 mg daily x 6-9 months	No

E. Paronychia

Pathophysiology
- **Most commonly** caused by **S. aureus**

Physical Exam
- Erythema, fluctuance, warmth of lateral nail fold

Management
- Antibiotics, warm soaks; incision and drainage if severe

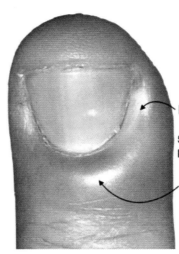

Paronychia

Soft tissue infection of **lateral** and **proximal nail folds**

Eponychia

Clinical
- *Staphylococcus aureus* or *Streptococcus*
- Fungal less common
- Can progress into pulp of fingertip (felon)

Management
- Warm soaks and antibiotics for mild cases
- Drainage of pus with elevation of nail skin fold
- Severe cases require incision and drainage

IV. Envenomations and Arthropod Bite Reactions

A. Scorpion, Spiders, Snakes

Organism	Location (USA)	Unique Physical Characteristics	Incidence of Toxicity	Classic Findings	Antivenin Available
Scorpion	Southwest	Tan colored	Frequent systemic sxs	• Fasciculations • Disconjugate gaze • Temperature reversal	Yes
Brown recluse	Midwest	Fiddle/Violin on dorsal cephalothorax	10% develop necrotic ulcer	• Papule to necrotic blister	No
Black widow	Nationwide	Red hourglass on ventral abdomen	Systemic sxs common	• Local papule with halo • Muscle fasciculations • Abdominal pain • Diaphoresis	Yes

Organism	Location (USA)	Unique Physical Characteristics	Incidence of Toxicity	Classic Findings	Antivenin Available
Pit viper	None in Maine, Alaska, Hawaii	Triangular head and elliptical pupils	75% positive for envenomation	• Local swelling • Oozing blood from wound • Coagulopathy	Yes
Eastern coral	Southwest	Red on yellow stripes with black in between	60% positive for envenomation	• Muscle paralysis	Yes

V. Exanthems

ERYTHEMA INFECTIOSUM (FIFTH DISEASE) • HAND, FOOT, AND MOUTH DISEASE • MEASLES

A. "Erythema" Rashes

Erythema multiforme
- Target-like lesions
- Infectious, medication, autoimmune

Erythema marginatum
- Macule with central clearing
- Spares the face
- Rheumatic fever

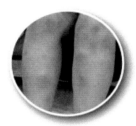

Erythema nodosum
- Inflammatory nodules
- Infectious, autoimmune, medication, pregnancy

Erythema migrans
- Bull's eye appearance
- Lyme disease

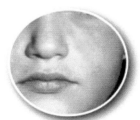

Erythema infectiosum
- Slapped cheek appearance
- Circumoral pallor
- Parvovirus B19 infection

B. Erythema Infectiosum (Fifth Disease)

Pathophysiology
- **Most commonly** caused by **parvovirus B19**

Patient
- History of **URI symptoms** 3 - 4 days prior of rash onset

Physical Exam
- **"Slapped cheek"** rash

Comments
- Complications may include **aplastic crisis** in sickle cell patients

 Human parvovirus B19

 Sickle cell patients at risk for Aplastic anemia

Coryza, headache, fever

Bright red facial rash "slapped cheek"

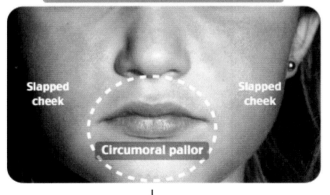

Slapped cheek | Slapped cheek

Circumoral pallor

Reticulated, lacelike rash on trunk & extremities

|

C. Hand, Foot and Mouth Disease

Pathophysiology
- **Most commonly** caused by **Coxsackievirus A**

Patient
- Child younger than five years of age

Presentation
- Decreased appetite and fever

Physical Exam
- **Oral exanthem** plus a **macular, maculopapular,** or **vesicular rash** on the **hands and feet**

Management
- Supportive care

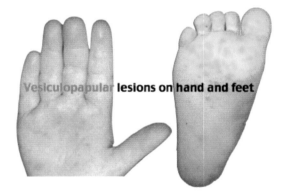

Vesiculopapular lesions on hand and feet

Clinical
- Mouth or throat pain (verbal children)
- Refusal to eat (non-verbal children)
- Fever
- Prodromal symptoms usually absent

Oral enanthem
Ulcers of anterior oral cavity (most common on tongue and buccal mucosa

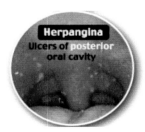

Herpangina
Ulcers of posterior oral cavity

D. Measles (Rubeola)

Patient
- **Unvaccinated** young child

Presentation
- High **fever, cough, conjunctivitis, coryza**
- **Maculopapular rash** starting on the **head** and spreading towards the **feet**

Physical Exam
- **Red spots** with **blue-white** center on **buccal mucosa** (Koplik spots)

Diagnostic Studies
- Diagnosis is made **clinically**

Management
- Supportive care

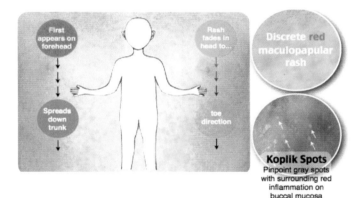

First appears on forehead

Spreads down trunk

Rash fades in head to...

toe direction

Discrete red maculopapular rash

Koplik Spots
Pinpoint gray spots with surrounding red inflammation on buccal mucosa

Clinical
- High fever
- Cough, Coryza, Conjunctivitis (The 3 C's)
- Rash
- Koplik spots

Complications
- Diarrhea (most common)
- Pneumonia (most common cause of mortality)
- Acute disseminated encephalomyelitis (ADEM)
- Subacute sclerosing panencephalitis (SSPE)

VI. Infectious Diseases

BACTERIAL • FUNGAL • PARASITIC • VIRAL

1. BACTERIAL

A. Cellulitis

Pathophysiology
- **Most commonly** caused by **S. aureus** and streptococci

Presentation
- **Pain, redness, swelling**

Physical Exam
- Tenderness, **erythema with poorly demarcated borders,** lymphedema

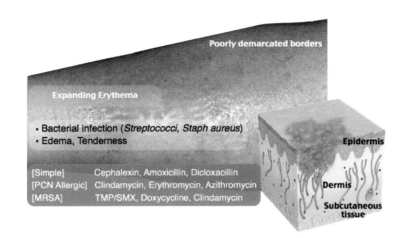

Poorly demarcated borders

Expanding Erythema

- Bacterial infection (*Streptococci, Staph aureus*)
- Edema, Tenderness

[Simple]	Cephalexin, Amoxicillin, Dicloxacillin
[PCN Allergic]	Clindamycin, Erythromycin, Azithromycin
[MRSA]	TMP/SMX, Doxycycline, Clindamycin

Epidermis

Dermis

Subcutaneous tissue

B. Erysipelas

Pathophysiology
- **Most commonly** caused by **Streptococcus pyogenes** infection (group A beta-hemolytic Strep)

Presentation
- Malaise, fever, chills, nausea

Physical Exam
- Intensely erythematous, **sharply demarcated, slightly raised** plaque

Management
- Penicillin V, amoxicillin, azithromycin, or clarithromycin

Erysipelas – Involves **upper dermis** and **superficial lymphatics**
Cellulitis – Involves **upper dermis** and **subcutaneous fat**

Clinical
- Tend to have acute onset with systemic manifestations
- Fever and chills
- Cellulitis tends to be more indolent

Management
- Elevation of affected area (e.g. limb)
- Ceftriaxone, cefazolin (systemic symptoms)
- Amoxicillin, cephalexin (mild ot moderate)

Erysipelas cont.

Most commonly caused by **Beta-hemolytic streptococci** (*Streptococcus* pyogenes)

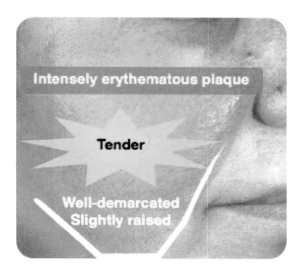

Intensely erythematous plaque

Tender

Well-demarcated
Slightly raised

Butterfly pattern

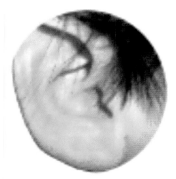

Milian Ear sign
Involvement of the ear
(No deeper dermis)

C. Impetigo

Pathophysiology
- **Most commonly** caused by **S. aureus** and *Streptococcus*

Patient
- Child younger than six years of age

Presentation
- **Non-painful**, **pruritic lesions** on face

Physical Exam
- **Honey-colored** weeping lesions with **crusting**

Management
- Topical **mupirocin**

Comments
- Complications include **poststreptococcal glomerulonephritis**

Microbiology
- *Staphylococcus aureus* (most common)
- Beta-hemolytic streptococci

1 Non-bullous impetigo

- Papules, vesicles, & pustules
- Rapidly break down
- Form golden adherent crusts
- Often located on face or extremities

2 Bullous impetigo

- Flaccid, fluid-filled bullae
- Rupture
- Leaves a thin brown crust
- Often located on trunk

3 Ecthyma

- "Punched-out" ulcers
- Overlying crust
- Raised violaceous borders

Treatment
- Limited: Topical **mupirocin** or retapamulin
- Extensive: Systemic antibiotics (dicloxacillin, cephalexin)
- If MRSA suspected: trimethoprim sulfamethoxazole

2. FUNGAL

A. Oropharyngeal Candidiasis (Thrush)

Pathophysiology
- **Most commonly** caused by *Candida albicans*

Physical Exam
- White plaques on tongue, palate, inner cheeks that **can be scraped off**

Management
- Topical **nystatin** or oral **fluconazole**

- Curd-like, creamy-white plaques overlying an erythematous mucosa

Candida albicans
- Plaques scrape off (unlike hairy leukoplakia)
- Rx: Antifungal (nystatin, clotrimazole, fluconazole)

B. Candidal Diaper Dermatitis

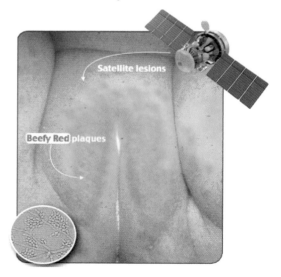

Satellite lesions

Beefy Red plaques

C. Dermatophyte Infections

KOH
- Long, branching, fungal hyphae with septations

Tinea Barbae
- Papules and pustules, around hair follicles

Tinea Pedis (Athlete's Foot)
- Pruritic scaly eruptions between toes
- Trichophyton rubrum is the most common dermatophyte causing athlete's foot
- Management: topical antifungals

|

Dermatophyte Infections cont.

Dermatophyte: *Trichophyton*

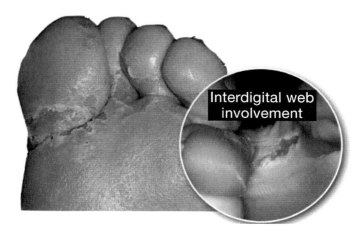

Transmitted in communal areas where people go barefoot
- Swimming pools
- Locker rooms

D. Tinea Cruris ("Jock Itch")
- Diffusely red rash in the groin or on the scrotum

Causes
- *Trichophyton robrum* (most common)
- *Epidermophyton floccosum*
- *Trichophyton interdigitale*

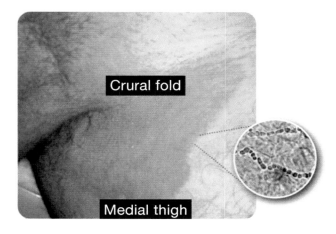

Clinical
- Begins with an erythematous patch on the proximal medial thigh
- Infection spreads centrifugally with partial central clearing
- Slightly elevated, sharply demarcated border
- Infection may spread to perineum, perianal, and into gluteal cleft
- Scrotum is typically spared in males

Diagnosis
- Potassium hydroxide (KOH) exam of scales scraped from lesion
- Segmented hyphae characteristic of dermatophyte infections

Treatment
- Topical therapy with anti-fungal
- Azoles (e.g. clotrimazole)
- Allylamines (e.g. terbinafine)
- Butenadine, ciclopirox, tolnaftate
- Nystatin is not effective

E. Tinea Capitis
- **Most common** fungal infection in the pediatric population
- Occurs mainly in prepubescent children (between ages 3 wand 7 years)
- Asymptomatic carriers are common and contribute to spread

Trichophyton and Microsporum spp. are most common cause

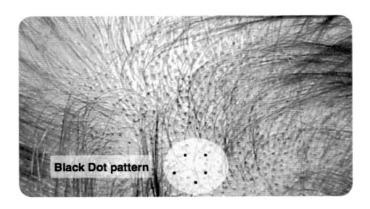

Black Dot pattern

Topical treatment is ineffective

Treatment
- Oral antifungal
- Griseofulvin (first-line)
- Terbinafine (alternative first-line)
- Fluconazole
- Itraconazole

F. Tinea Corporis ("Ringworm")
- Usually seen in younger children or in young adolescents with close physical contact with others (Ex: wrestlers)

Trichophyton rubrum is most common cause

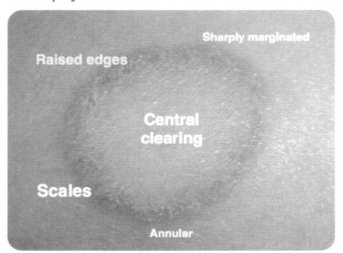

Sharply marginated
Raised edges
Central clearing
Scales
Annular

Granuloma annulare
- A benign inflammatory condition
- No epidermal involvement
- **NON-SCALING**

3. PARASITIC

A. Pediculosis Capitis (Head Lice)

Pathophysiology
- Caused by ***Pediculus humanus capiti*s**

Patient
- Child

Presentation
- Scalp itching

Physical Exam
- Nits (eggs) or actual lice

Management
- Topical pediculicides, such as **permethrin**

Comments
- A second treatment should be applied on **day nine** after the first treatment to ensure eradication

Head louse
Pediculus humanus capitis

Pediculosis Capitis (Head Lice) cont.

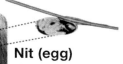

Nit (egg)
- Hatch in 8 days
- Release nymphs
- Nymphs become adults

Transmission
- Direct contact with head of infested person
- Lice do not jump, fly, or use pets as vectors

Treatment
- Wet combing (young infants)
- Topical pediculicides
  - Permethrin
  - Malathion
  - Benzyl alcohol
  - Spinosad
  - Topical ivermectin

Clinical
- Pruritus (reaction to saliva injected during feeding)

B. Scabies

Pathophysiology
- **Most commonly** caused by *Sarcoptes scabiei hominis*

Presentation
- **Severe pruritus** that is worse at night

Physical Exam
- Small papules, **vesicles, and linear burrows in the webbed spaces of the fingers and toes**

Diagnostic Studies
- Microscopic visualization

Management
- **Permethrin**

Treatment
Eradication of mites
- Permethrin 5% cream (safe for infants)
- Oval Ivermectin (ideal for nursing home outbreaks)

1 Mite lays eggs and drops feces

2 Type IV hypersensitivity reaction
Intense pruritus
Worse at night

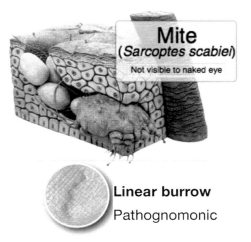

Mite
(Sarcoptes scabiei)
Not visible to naked eye

Linear burrow
Pathognomonic

Clinical - Rash
- Small, erythematous, nondescript papule
- Often excoriated, hemorrhagic crusts

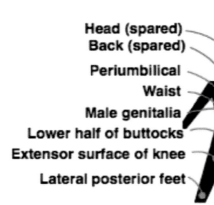

Head (spared)
Back (spared)
Periumbilical
Waist
Male genitalia
Lower half of buttocks
Extensor surface of knee
Lateral posterior feet

Skin immediately adjacent to nipples
Anterior and posterior axillary folds
Extensor aspects of elbow
Flexor aspects of wrist
Sides and webs of fingers

Head (involved in children)

4. VIRAL

A. Condyloma Acuminata

Pathophysiology
- **Most commonly** caused by **HPV 6 & 11**

Presentation
- Genital lesions

Physical Exam
- **Cauliflower-like** lesion

Comments
- **Most common STI**

Anogenital warts

Most common sexually transmitted infection in the world

Human papillomavirus
HPV types 6 and 11 most common

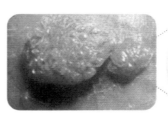

Treatment

Patient-applied
- Imiquimod
- Podophyllotoxin
- Sinecatechins

Clinician-administered
- Cryotherapy
- Trichloroacetic acid
- Surgical removal

Cauliflower-like lesions

Warts can be: **single or multiple, flat, dome-shaped, cauliflower-shaped, filiform, fungating, pedunculated, cerebriform, plaque-like, smooth** (especially on the penile shaft), **verrucous,** or **lobulated**

B. Herpes Simplex Labialis

Pathophysiology
- **Most commonly** caused by **HSV type 1 (HSV type 2** implicated in genital lesions)

Presentation
- **Painful** oral lesions

Physical Exam
- Tender vesicles and erosions on the **tongue**, **buccal mucosa**, and **lips**

Diagnostic Studies
- Diagnosis made **clinically**
- Gold standard diagnosis is tissue culture with polymerase chain reaction (**PCR**)
- **Tzanck smear** will show **multinucleated giant cells**

Management
- Topical antiviral therapy or oral **acyclovir**

C. Herpetic Gingivostomatitis

Most common manifestation of primary herpes simplex virus infection during childhood

HSV Type 1

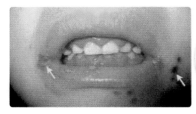
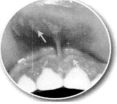

Ulcerative lesions of the **gingiva** and **mucous membranes** of the mouth, with **perioral vesicular lesions**

Complications
- Dehydration (most common)
- Herpetic whitlow or keratisis
- Secondary bacteremia
- Esophagitis
- Eczema herpeticum

Management
- Supportive care
- Acyclovir (within 72 to 96 hours of symptoms)

Clinical
- Most common between 6 months and 5 years of age
- Usually from direct contact of oral secretions
- Begins with prodrome of fever, irritability, anorexia, malaise

D. Genital Herpes

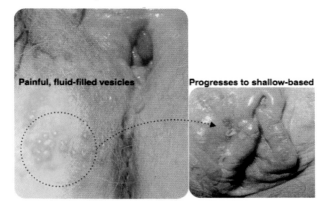

Painful, fluid-filled vesicles

Progresses to shallow-based

Treatment
- Acyclovir
- Famciclovir
- Valacyclovir

Clinical – primary infection
- Systemic symptoms (fever, headache, malaise)
- Local pain and itching
- Dysuria
- Tender lymphadenopathy

E. Molluscum Contagiosum

Pathophysiology
- **Most commonly** caused by **Poxvirus**

Patient
- School-aged child
- History of HIV/AIDS

Presentation
- Complaining of "warts"

Physical Exam
- Multiple **waxy**, dome-shaped papules with **umbilicated** appearance

Management
- Lesions are self-limiting though **curettage** or other topical management can be utilized

Clinical
- Most common in school-age children
- Transmitted by direct contact
- Painless, no systemic symptoms
- Typically affects face, torso, extremities
- Spares the palms and soles

Management
- Resolves spontaneously (no therapy needed)
- Cryotherapy
- Curettage
- Cantharidin
- Podophyllotoxin

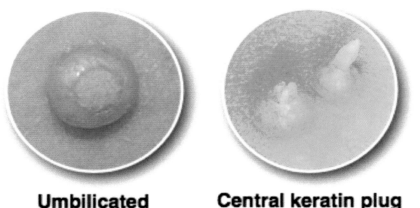

Umbilicated **Central keratin plug** **Poxvirus**

F. Varicella (Chickenpox)

Presentation
- Viral prodrome and maculopapular rash

Physical Exam
- Clear vesicles on an erythematous base ("**dew drop on a rose petal**" rash)
- Crops of lesions in **multiple stages**

Management
- < 12-years-old: supportive care
- > 12-years-old: acyclovir

Treatment
- **Healthy ≤ 12 years of age:** Self-limited, supportive care
- **Immunocompromised** or **> 12:** Acyclovir

Severe complication
- Pneumonitis
- Encephalitis

Vaccine
- Live attenuated
- Avoid in pregnancy

First vesicle appears

Crops of vesicles in various stages of healing

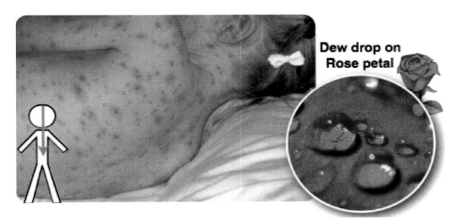

Dew drop on Rose petal

RASH
Starts at **hairline**
Spreads inferiorly to chest, palms, soles

G. Herpes Zoster (Shingles)

Pathophysiology
- **Most commonly** caused by reactivation of latent **varicella-zoster virus**

Patient
- Elderly

Presentation
- Painful, papulovesicular rash **preceded by tingling** or **hyperesthesia**

Physical Exam
- Rash with unilateral dermatomal distribution that **does not cross midline**

Diagnostic Studies
- **Tzanck smear** will reveal **multinucleated giant cells**

Management
- Acyclovir

 Varicella-zoster virus

Clinical
- Rash
- Acute neuritis (pain)

Complications
- Postherpetic neuralgia (8%)
- Bacterial skin infection (2%)
- Uveitis/Keratitis (1.5%)
- Motor neuropathy (1%)
- Meningitis (0.5%)
- Zoster oticus (0.2%)

Comments
- **Postherpetic neuralgia**: persistent pain > three months
- **Vaccination** indicated at age 60

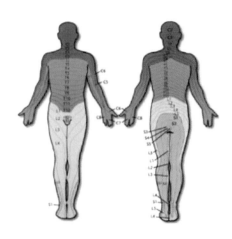

Dermatomal distribution

(Thoracic/Lumbar most common)

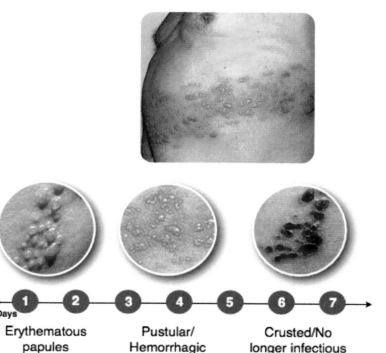

Days 1 2 3 4 5 6 7

Erythematous papules | Pustular/ Hemorrhagic | Crusted/No longer infectious

H. Verruca Plantaris (Plantar Warts)

<u>Pathophysiology</u>
- **Most commonly** caused by **HPV type 1**

<u>Presentation</u>
- Painful lesion on soles of feet

<u>Physical Exam</u>
- Hyperkeratotic lesion with black dots

<u>Management</u>
- Salicylic acid or cryotherapy

Management
- Spontaneous resolution (more common in children)
- Salicylic acid (first line)
- Cryotherapy (first line)
- Bleomycin
- Trichloroacetic acid
- Imiquimod

Human papillomavirus
HPV type 1 (soles of feet)
HPV 6 and 11 (anogenital)

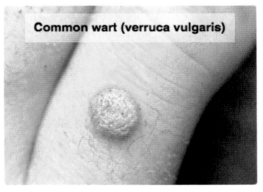

Common wart (verruca vulgaris)

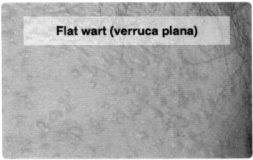

Flat wart (verruca plana)

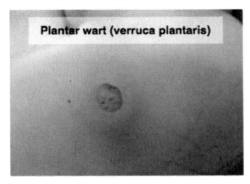

Plantar wart (verruca plantaris)

VII. Keratotic Disorders

ACTINIC KERATOSIS • SEBORRHEIC KERATOSIS

A. Actinic Keratosis

Patient
- Man with a history of an **outdoor occupation** and **sun exposure**

Presentation
- Rough bumps on head

Physical Exam
- **Rough**, **scaly**, **erythematous** papules on sun-exposed areas

Comments
- Precancerous for **squamous cell carcinoma**

Risk Factor
- UV radiation
- Fair-skinned individuals
- Sun exposed areas

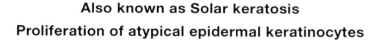

Precancerous for **Squamous cell carcinoma**

Also known as Solar keratosis
Proliferation of atypical epidermal keratinocytes

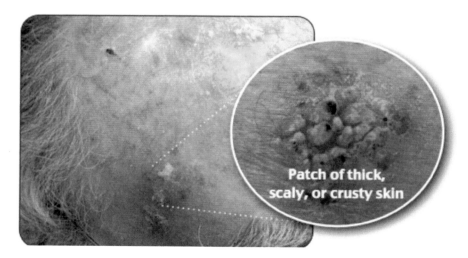

Patch of thick, scaly, or crusty skin

|

B. Seborrheic Keratosis

Patient

- Older individuals, often elderly

Physical Exam

- A lesion, flat or raised, smooth or velvety with "stuck-on" appearance noted on the face, shoulders, chest, or back

Treatment

- Liquid nitrogen, curretage, shave removal

Comments

- Most commonly caused by a benign, epidermal neoplasm

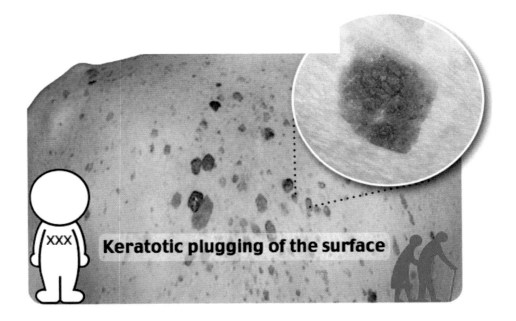

Keratotic plugging of the surface

VIII. Neoplasms

BENIGN • MALIGNANT • PREMALIGNANT

A. Melanoma

Patient
- Fair-skinned with history of **severe blistering sunburns** and family history of melanoma or dysplastic nevus syndrome

Presentation
- Itching, painful lesion that **won't heal**

Physical Exam
- Ulcerated lesion and **ABCDE**
  - **A**symmetry
  - **B**order irregularity
  - **C**olor variation
  - **D**iameter
  - **E**volution

Diagnostic Studies
- Biopsy: excisional or punch
- **Depth** is most important factor (Breslow's depth)

Management
- **Excision** with adequate margins; **interferon** reduces recurrence

B. ABCDEs of Melanoma

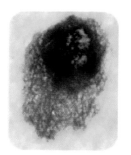   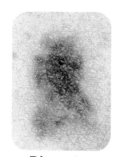 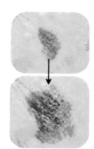

| Asymmetry | Border Irregularity | Color Variations | Diameter (≥ 6 mm or 1/4 inch) | Evolution |

C. Squamous Cell Carcinoma

Patient
- History of **HPV**, chronic sun exposure, exposure to arsenic or radiation

Presentation
- Non-healing lesion that sometimes bleeds

Physical Exam
- Red, scaly, hyperkeratotic nodular, papule or plaque that does not itch.
- Most common on lips, hands, neck, head (**sun-exposed areas**)

Diagnostic Studies
- Clinical exam, skin biopsy confirms

Management
- Wide local **excision**, radiation therapy

Comments
- Second most common skin cancer
- **Actinic keratosis** is a precursor

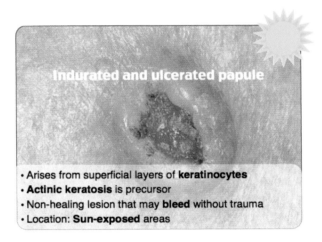

Indurated and ulcerated papule

- Arises from superficial layers of **keratinocytes**
- **Actinic keratosis** is precursor
- Non-healing lesion that may **bleed** without trauma
- Location: **Sun-exposed** areas

D. Basal Cell Carcinoma

<u>Presentation</u>
- Painless, slow-growing lesion on the face, ears, or neck

<u>Physical Exam</u>
- **Pearly papule** with **rolled borders** and **telangiectasia**

<u>Diagnostic Studies</u>
- Shave biopsy

<u>Management</u>
- Surgical excision

<u>Comments</u>
- **Most common** skin cancer

Squamos Cell Carcinoma
- Arises from superficial layers of keratinocytes
- Actinic keratosis is precursor
- Non-healing lesion that may bleed without trauma
- Location: Sun-exposed areas

Most common skin cancer in USA

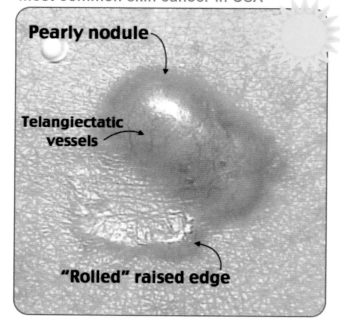

Pearly nodule

Telangiectatic vessels

"Rolled" raised edge

Actinic Keratosis
- Also known as solar keratosis
- Atypical epidermal keratinocytes
- Precancerous for squamous cell

Melanoma
- Asymmetry
- Boarder irregularity
- Color variations
- Diameter > 6 mm

Basal Cell Carcinoma
- Most common skin cancer (USA)
- Pearly nodule
- "Rolled" raised edge
- Telangiectactic vessels

|

E. Kaposi Sarcoma

Pathophysiology

- **Most commonly** caused by human herpesvirus 8 (**HHV-8**)

Patient

- History of HIV infection

Physical Exam

- Nodules, plaques, and papules that are black, purple, or red in color

Diagnostic Studies

- CD4 counts **< 200 cells/mm3**
- Biopsy is diagnostic (presence of **spindle cells**)

Comments

- This is an **AIDS-defining** illness

Clinical

- Purplish, reddish blue or dark brown/black macules, plaques, and nodules
- Nodular lesions may ulcerate and bleed

Kaposi sarcoma-associated herpesvirus (KSHV)
aka Human herpesvirus 8 (HHV-8)

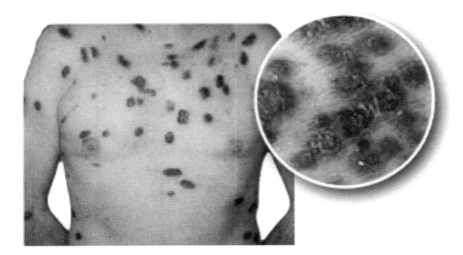

IX. Papulosquamous Disorders

CONTACT DERMATITIS • DRUG ERUPTIONS • ECZEMA
LICHEN PLANUS • PITYRIASIS ROSEA • PSORIASIS

A. Allergic Contact Dermatitis

• Well-demarcated erythema, erosions, vesicles

T-cell mediated, delayed-type hypersensitivity response to exogenous agents

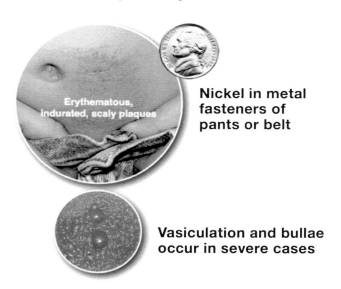

Erythematous, indurated, scaly plaques

Nickel in metal fasteners of pants or belt

Vasiculation and bullae occur in severe cases

Other common causes
• Urushiol (Poison ivy)
• Cobalt
• Potassium dichromate

B. Drug Eruptions

Pathophysiology
• An adverse cutaneous reaction in response to administration of a drug
• Severity can range from mild eruptions that

resolve after the removal of the inciting agent to severe skin damage with multiorgan involvement

Comments
• Skin reactions are the **most common** adverse drug reactions

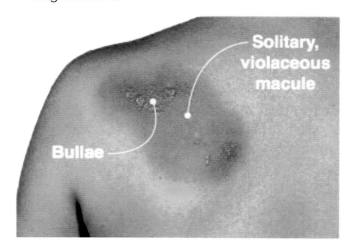

Solitary, violaceous macule

Bullae

Eliciting Drugs
• Trimethoprim-sulfamethoxazole, tetracyclines, penicillins, quinolones, dapsone
• NSAIDs, acetylsalicylic acid
• Acetaminophen
• Antimalarials

Clinical
• Systemic symptoms are usually absent
• Pruritus and a burning or stinging sensation are common
• May occur anywhere on body

Management
• Drug withdrawal and avoidance
• Supportive care (e.g. diphenhydramine)

C. Atopic Dermatitis (Eczema)

<u>Patient</u>
- History of **asthma** or **allergic rhinitis**

<u>Presentation</u>
- **Itchy**, **scaly** rash often worse in the winter

<u>Physical Exam</u>
- Thick, leathery, hyperpigmented areas on **flexor** surfaces

<u>Management</u>

Sine qua non → PRURITIS
Vicious cycle of itch-scratch-rash-itch

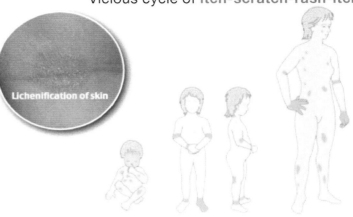

Cheeks Trunk　　**Flexor surfaces**　　**Hands**

D. Nummular Eczema (Discoid Eczema)

- Coin-shaped/discoid plaques

Clinical
- Highly pruritic, round, coin-shaped patches (1 to 10 cm in diameter)
- Acute: lesions are dull red, exudative, and crusted
- Over time: dry, scaly, with occasional central clearing
- Legs and upper extremities most commonly involved
- Chronic and relapsing

Management
- Measures to reduce skin dryness and exposure to irritants
- Corticosteroids
- Phototherapy (severe or refractory)
- Methotrexate, cyclosporin

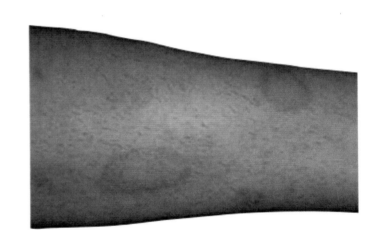

Coin-shaped lesions

E. Acute Palmoplantar Eczema (Dyshidrotic Eczema)

Presentation
- **Intense pruritus** on palms and sides of **fingers**

Physical Exam
- Deep vesicles with "**tapioca-like**" appearance

Management
- Avoid long exposure to water
- **Topical corticosteroids** for acute flares

Previously kown as dyshidrotic eczema

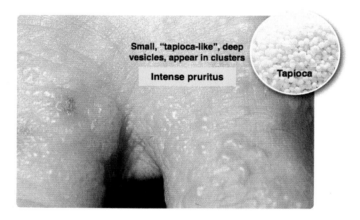

Small, "tapioca-like", deep vesicles, appear in clusters
Intense pruritus
Tapioca

Management
- Avoid irritants or exacerbating factors
- General skin care
- Topic corticosteroids
- Topical calcineurin inhibitors
- Systemic corticosteroids (severe disease)

F. Lichen Planus

Presentation
- Pruritic skin discolorations on ankles or wrists

Physical Exam
- **P**ruritic, **p**urple, **p**olygonal, and **p**apules (**four P's**) and fine, white lines (**Wickham's striae**)

Management
- **Corticosteroids**

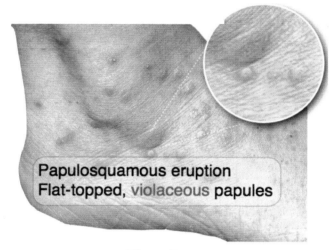

Papulosquamous eruption
Flat-topped, violaceous papules

The 4 Ps
- Pruritic
- Purple
- Polygonal
- Papules

Clinical
- Most common between ages 30 and 60
- Autoimmune
- May affect skin, mucous membranes (oral mucosa), scalp, nails, genitalia

Management
- Corticosteroids

G. Lichen Simplex Chronicus

Presentation
- Generalized pruritus and frequent scratching

Physical Exam
- Multiple **linear excoriations** and **thickened skin**

Management
- Aimed at reducing pruritus and **minimizing rubbing and scratching**

Neurodermatitis

due to **chronic itching** and **scratching**

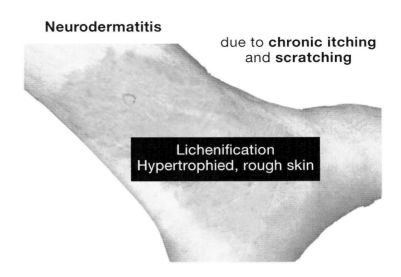

Lichenification
Hypertrophied, rough skin

H. Pityriasis Rosea

Patient
- History of large, oval, scaly patch one week prior "Herald Patch"

Presentation
- Rash on **back**

Physical Exam
- Diffuse papulosquamous rash on trunk with "**Christmas tree-like**" distribution

Management
- Self-limiting disease; treat itching with antihistamines

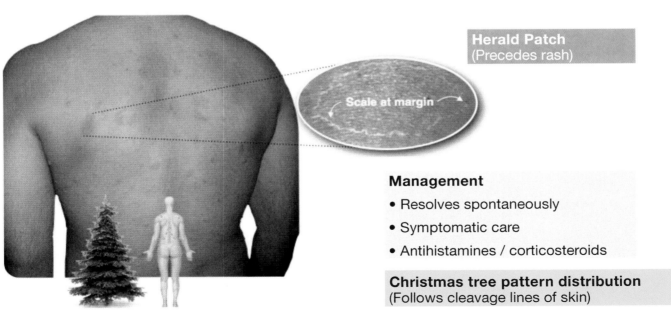

Herald Patch
(Precedes rash)

Scale at margin

Management
- Resolves spontaneously
- Symptomatic care
- Antihistamines / corticosteroids

Christmas tree pattern distribution
(Follows cleavage lines of skin)

I. Psoriasis

<u>Presentation</u>
  • Rash on **extensor** surfaces of arms and legs

<u>Physical Exam</u>
  • **Nail pitting** and bilateral, sharply marginated papules and plaques with **silvery scales**
  • **Positive** Auspitz sign (scale removal produces blood droplets)

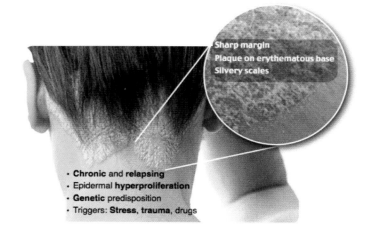

- **Chronic** and **relapsing**
- Epidermal **hyperproliferation**
- **Genetic** predisposition
- Triggers: **Stress, trauma**, drugs

Clinical

• Bimodal distribution

• Early onset predicts more serious course

• Well-demarcated erythematous plaques

• Plaques covered by waxy, silvery-white scales

• Bilateral involvement of extensor surfaces, scalp, palms, and soles

• Nail pitting

• Auspitz phenomenon - removal of scale results in pinpoint blood droplet

• Koebner phenomenon - disease occurs at sites of trauma

• Guttate psoriasis - follows a streptococcal infection

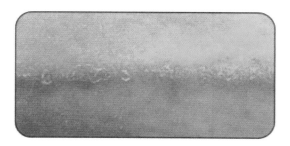

Koebner phenomenon
Plaque formation on site of **prior trauma** 1-2 weeks after skin injury

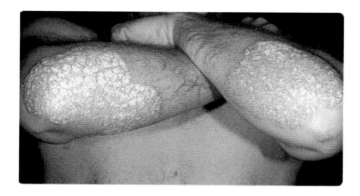

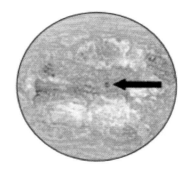

Auspitz's sign
The appearance of punctate bleeding spots when psoriasis scales are scraped off

J. Guttate Psoriasis

<u>Pathophysiology</u>
- **Most commonly** caused by
preceding **streptococcal** infection

<u>Presentation</u>
- **Acute eruption** of numerous small,
erythematous papules and plaques

<u>Physical Exam</u>
- "**Drop-like**" appearance of skin lesions

Management
- Ultraviolet phototherapy
- Topical corticosteroids and vitamin D analogs

Often a preceding history of
streptococcal infection

Guttate refers
to "**drop-like**"
appearance

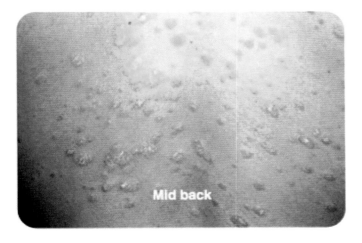

Mid back

X. Pigment Disorders

MELASMA • VITILIGO

A. Melasma

Pathophysiology
- **Most commonly** caused by hormonal changes

Patient
- Woman who is **pregnant** or using **oral contraceptives**

Presentation
- **Discoloration** on parts of face

Physical Exam
- Dark, irregular, well-demarcated, **hyperpigmented** macules and patches

Management
- Sunscreen and sun avoidance

Comments
- Termed **chloasma** during pregnancy

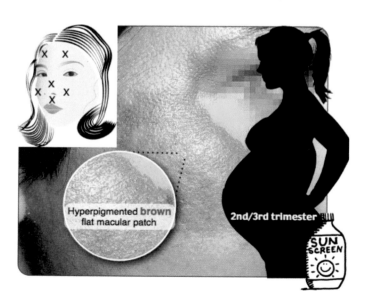

Hyperpigmented brown flat macular patch

2nd/3rd trimester

B. Vitiligo

Pathophysiology
- **Most commonly** caused by **autoimmune destruction** of melanocytes

Presentation
- **Patches** of **pale skin** affecting the **neck**, **upper back**, and **chest**

Physical Exam
- **Non-scaling**, **well-demarcated** areas of **hypopigmentation**

Diagnostic Studies
- **Wood's lamp** exam will accentuate the hypopigmentation

Depigmentation of the skin

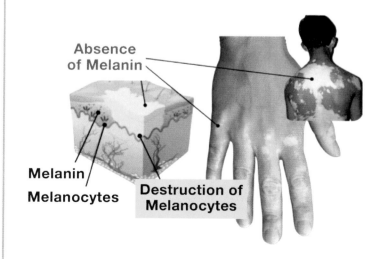

Absence of Melanin

Melanin

Melanocytes

Destruction of Melanocytes

Frequently Associated with Autoimmune Thyroid Disease

- Alopecia areata
- Psoriasis
- Type 1 diabetes
- Rheumatoid arthritisd
- Inflammatory bowel disease
- Pernicious anemia
- Myasthenia gravis
- Lupus
- Sjögren syndrome

Management

- Psychosocial support

Stabilization

- Oral corticosteroids, NB-UVB phototherapy
- Minocycline, methotrexate, vitamin supplementation

Regimentation

- Topic corticosteroids, calcineurin inhibitors, vitamin D analogues
- Phototherapy

C. Tinea Versicolor (Pityriasis Versicolor)

Pathophysiology
- **Most commonly** caused by *Malassezia furfur*

Presentation
- Hypopigmented areas that do not tan

Physical Exam
- Scaly patches on the chest and trunk

Diagnostic Studies
- Diagnosis is made by KOH preparation of skin scraping

Management
- Treatment is topical **selenium sulfide**

NOT a dermatophyte infection
Caused by saprophytic, lipid-dependent yeasts

Malassezia (genus) [formerly known as *Pityosporum*]

Clinical
- Involves trunk and extremities
- Typically hypopigmented
- Can be hyperpigmented or erythematous

Diagnosis
- Potassium hydroxide (KOH) prep
- Spaghetti and meatballs appearance

Management
- Topical antifungals
- Oral antifungal therapy (for severe or recalcitrant)

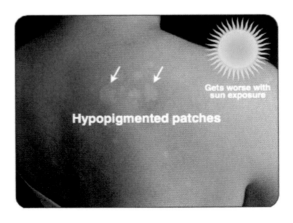

Gets worse with sun exposure
Hypopigmented patches

XI. Skin Integrity

BURNS • LACERATIONS • PRESSURE ULCERS • STASIS DERMATITIS

A. Burns

Burn Classification				
Clinical appearance	Thickness	Degree	Depth	Characteristics
	Superficial	1st	Epidermis	Pain, redness, mild swelling
	Superficial Partial	2nd	Dermis: papillary region	Pain, blisters, splotchy skin, severe swelling
	Deep partial		Dermis: reticular region	White, leathery, relatively painless
	Full	3rd	Hypodermis (subcutaneous tissue)	Charred, insensate, eschar formation

B. Rule of Nines

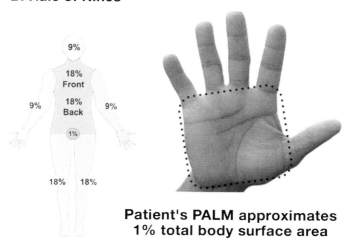

9%
18% Front
9%   18% Back   9%
1%
18%   18%

**Patient's PALM approximates
1% total body surface area**

C. Lacerations

Anatomic site	Suture Removal
Eyelids	3 days
Neck	3 to 4 days
Face	5 days
Scalp	7 to 14 days
Trunk and upper extremities	7 days
Lower extremities	8 to 10 days
Joints	10 to 14 days

D. Pressure Ulcer Stages

Stage 1	Stage 2	Stage 3	Stage 4
Non-blanchable erythema	Partial thickness	Full thickness skin loss	Full thickness tissue loss

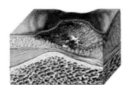

Stage 1 / Stage 2 diagram labels: Skin, Adipose, Muscle/tendon, Bone

- Intact skin
- May be painful

- Shallow open ulcer
- Red/pink wound bed

- Subcutaneous fat may be visible
- Bone, muscle, tendon not exposed
- May include tunneling

- Exposed bone, tendon, or muscle
- Slough or eschar may be present
- Undermining and tunneling

E. Stasis Dermatitis

Patient
- History of **poor circulation**

Physical Exam
- Swelling spreads beyond the ankle to the calf
- Dry, cracked, itchy skin
- Red to violet-colored open sores (medical term: venous ulcer), which can appear on the lower legs and tops of the feet
- Sores leak fluid and scab as they heal
- **Shiny**, atophic, **hairless** skin

Management
- Local wound care
- Compression therapy
- Skin grafting (if unhealed after 12 months of therapy)

Clinical
- Location between the knee and ankle
- Medial and lateral malleoli are the most common sites
- Pain is not severe
- Hyperpigmentation, lipodermatosclerosis, and stasis dermatitis

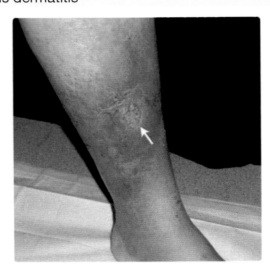

XII. Vesiculobullous Disease

PEMPHIGOID • PEMPHIGUS

A. Bullous Pemphigod

Pathophysiology
- **Most commonly** caused by a chronic autoimmune blistering disease

Patient
- Age > **60 years old**

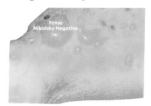

- **Autoimmune** disease of **elderly**
- Autoantibodies against basement membrane
- Subepidermal
- Begins as **pruritic papules**
- Large, **tense** blisters/bullae
- Older (>60 years) individuals
- Nikolsky **negative**

Presentation
- **Intensely pruritic papules** that become large, tense **blisters** and **bullae**

Physical Exam
- **Tense** and **firm** blisters that do not extend with lateral pressure (Negative Nikolsky sign)

Management
- **Corticosteroids** and **immunosuppressants**

Pemphigus vulgaris
- **Younger** (40-60 years)
- Involves **mucous membranes**
- **Flaccid** blisters
- Nikolsky **positive**

B. Pemphigus Vulgaris

Pathophysiology
- **Most common** cause is autoimmune

Patient
- Age **40-60 years old**

Presentation
- **Painful, flaccid bullae** on mucosal surfaces

Physical Exam
- Flaccid blisters that extend with lateral pressure (**Positive** Nikolsky sign)

Diagnostic Studies
- Tissue biopsy

Management
- High-dose **corticosteroids**

Clinical

- Mucous membrane lesions precede skin lesions
- Oral and esophageal mucous membrane involvement
- Dysphagia, hoarse voice, dehydration
- Painful, flaccid bullae

Management

- Admission
- Steroids
- Immune modulators (azathioprine, cyclophosphamide)
- High mortality rate if untreated

Etiology

- IgG against keratinocytes in desmosomes causes acantholysis
- Loss of cell-to-cell adhesion

Autoimmune mucocutaneous **intraepithelial bullous** disease

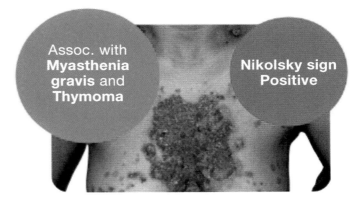

Assoc. with **Myasthenia gravis** and **Thymoma**

Nikolsky sign Positive

Epidermal separation with slight lateral pressure

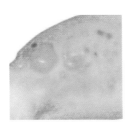

Bullous pemphigoid

- **Autoimmune** disease of **elderly**
- **Sub**epidermal
- Large **tense blisters**
- Nikolsky **negative**

	Pemphigus vulgaris	Bullous pemphigoid
Appearance	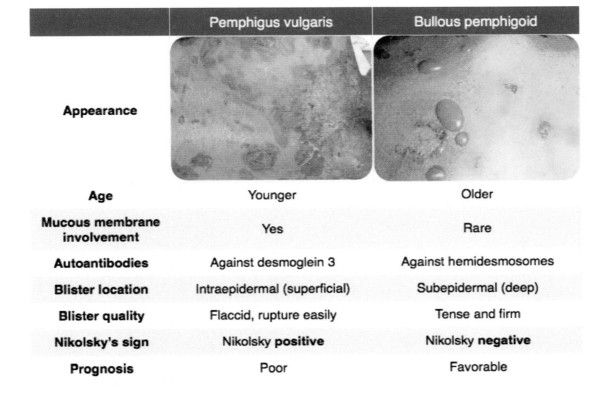	
Age	Younger	Older
Mucous membrane involvement	Yes	Rare
Autoantibodies	Against desmoglein 3	Against hemidesmosomes
Blister location	Intraepidermal (superficial)	Subepidermal (deep)
Blister quality	Flaccid, rupture easily	Tense and firm
Nikolsky's sign	Nikolsky **positive**	Nikolsky **negative**
Prognosis	Poor	Favorable

XIII. Other Dermatologic Disorders

ACANTHOSIS NIGRICANS • HIDRADENITIS SUPPURATIVA • LIPOMAS/EPIDERMAL INCLUSION CYSTS
PHOTOSENSITIVITY REACTIONS • PILONIDAL DISEASE • URTICARIA

A. Acanthosis Nigricans

Patient
- Obese or diabetic

Physical Exam
- Thickened, **velvety**, **darkly pigmented** plaques on **neck** or **axilla**

Comments
- Screen for **diabetes** in those not yet diagnosed

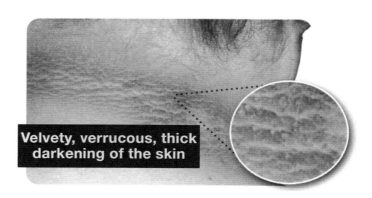

Velvety, verrucous, thick darkening of the skin

Etiology
- Obesity
- Endocrine and metabolic disorders (insulin resistance)
- Genetic syndromes
- Familial acanthosis nigricans
- Malignancy
- Drug reactions

B. Hidradenitis Suppurativa

Patient
- **Woman** with a history of lesions that have waxed and waned over several yearss

Presentation
- **Painful nodules** in **axillary** and **anogenital** area

Physical Exam
- **Tender, malodorous** lesions, often with **exudative drainage** and **sinus tracts**

Management
- **Intralesional triamcinolone**, topical clindamycin

Comments
- **Hurley staging system** describes severity of disease

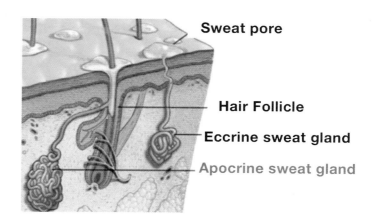

Sweat pore

Hair Follicle

Eccrine sweat gland

Apocrine sweat gland

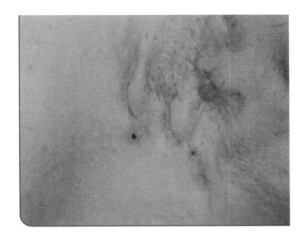

- Chronic
- Clusters of abscesses, epidermoid cysts, sebaceous cysts, pilonidal cysts
- Affects APOCRINE sweat glands
- Axilla, under breasts, inner thigh, groin, buttocks
- Triggers: Sweating, Hormonal changes related to menstrual cycle, Friction
- Persistent lesions lead to sinus tracts

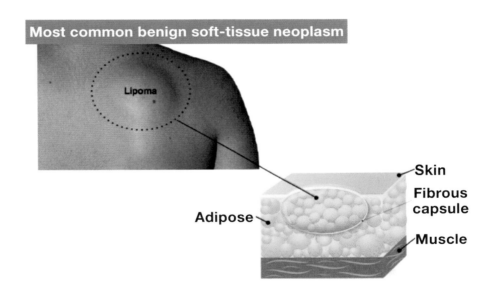

Most common benign soft-tissue neoplasm

Lipoma

Skin
Fibrous capsule
Adipose
Muscle

C. Lipoma

Pathophysiology
- Benign fatty tumor
- Type depends on histology

Patient
- Mostly in adults, M > F

Management
- Excision

D. Epidermal Inclusion Cyst (Sebaceous cyst)

Management
- Incision and drainage
- Excision (definitive)

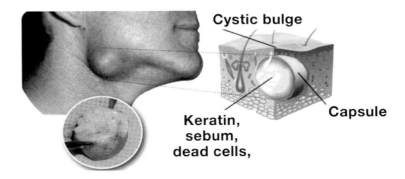

Cystic bulge

Keratin, sebum, dead cells,

Capsule

E. Pilonidal Disease

<u>Patient</u>

- **Man < 40 years old**

<u>Presentation</u>

- Painful area ovrer tailbone

<u>Physical Exam</u>

- **Tender**, **fluctuant** area in the **sacrococcygeal cleft**

<u>Management</u>

- **Acute**: incision and draingae
- **Definitive**: surgical excision

Management

- Incision and drainage (acute)
- Surgical excision (definitive)

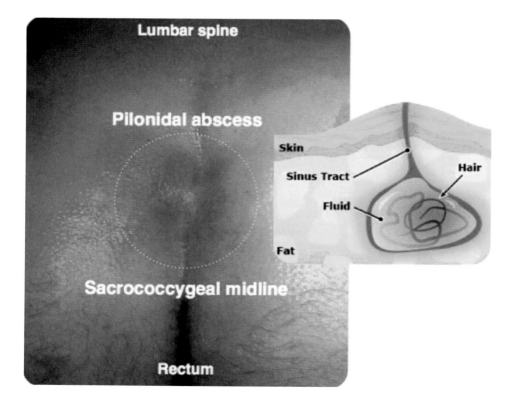

F. Urticaria

Presentation

- **Blanchable**, edematous, pink papules, wheals, or plaques
- **Angioedema**: painless, deeper form of urticaria affecting the lips, tongue, eyelids, hands, and genitals

Physical Exam

- Darier's sign: localized urticaria appearing where the skin is rubbed (histamine release)

Management

- If anaphylaxis: **epinephrine** 0.3–0.5 mg; use 1:1,000 dilution for IM route and 1:10,000 for IV route (Peds: epinephrine 0.01 mg/kg SC/IV)

Management
- Supportive care
- Antihistamines
- Glucocorticoids

Common Causes of Urticaria		
Drugs	• Penicillin • Sulfa • Aspirin • Local anesthetics • Diuretics	• NSAIDs • Morphine • Codeine • Progesterone
Infection	• Epstein-Barr virus • Hepatitis B virus	• Coxsackie virus • Parasitic infections
Environmental	• Heat • Cold • Exercise	• Metals • Animal saliva
Food	• Fish • Eggs • Nuts	• Shellfish • Fruits
Other	• Latex • Pregnancy • Malignancy	

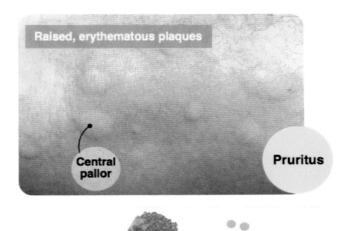

Raised, erythematous plaques

Central pallor

Pruritus

Allergen + Mast cell → Histamine release

Abbreviations

BB	Beta Blocker	**ESR**	Erythrocyte Sedimentation Rate
CCB	Calcium Channel Blocker	**ASAP**	As Soon As Possible
HTN	Hypertension	**CRP**	C-Reactive Protein
BP	Blood Pressure	**DVT**	Deep Vein Thrombosis
HR	Heart Rate	**NSAID**	Non-Steroidal Antiinflammatory
ACE	Angiotensin-Converting Enzyme	**HPV**	Human Papillomavirus
ACEI	Angiotensin-Converting Enzyme Inhibitor	**STI**	Sexually Transmitted Infection
ARB	Angiotensin II Receptor Blocker	**HSV**	Herpes Simplex Virus
CKD	Chronic Kidney Disease	**PCR**	Polymerase Chain Reaction
MI	Myocardial Infarction	**HIV**	Human Immunodeficiency Virus
HDL	High-Density Lipoprotein	**AIDS**	Acquired Immunodeficiency Syndrome
LDL	Low-Density Lipoprotein	**HHV**	Human Herpesvirus
ECG	Electrocardiogram	**CD4**	Cluster Of Differentiation 4
JVD	Jugular Venous Distension	**KOH**	Potassium Hydroxide
HTN	Hypertension	**URI**	Upper Respiratory Infection
CHF	Congestive Heart Failure	**CN**	Cranial Nerve
EF	Ejection Fraction	**TM**	Tympanic Membrane
LLSB	Lower Left Sternal Border	**HCTZ**	Hydrochlorothiazide
RUQ	Right Upper Quadrant	**Ig**	Immunoglobulin
CT	Computerized Tomography	**IM**	Intramuscular
AAA	Abdominal Aortic Aneurysm	**I&D**	Incision And Drainage
CTA	Computerized Tomography Angiography	**PCN**	Penicillin
MRA	Magnetic Resonance Angiography	**HIDA**	Hepatic Iminodiacetic Acid
MRI	Magnetic Resonance Imaging	**AMS**	Altered Mental Status
AVM	Arteriovenous Malformation	**ASCA**	Antibodies Against The Yeast *Saccharomyces Cerevisiae*

ANCA	Anti-Neutrophil Cytoplasmic Antibodies	**VCUG**	Voiding Cystourethrogram
p-ANCA	Perinuclear Anti-Neutrophil Cytoplasmic Antibodies	**UA**	Urinalysis
		TMP-SMX	Trimethoprim-Sulfamethoxazole
GI	Gastrointestinal	**CVA**	Costovertebral Angle
IBS	Irritable Bowel Syndrome	**CVA**	Cerebrovascular Accident
A-Fib	Atrial Fibrillation	**UVJ**	Ureterovesicular Junction
CAD	Coronary Artery Disease	**LDH**	Lactate Dehydrogenase
FAP	Familial Adenomatous Polyposis	**PT**	Prothrombin Time
CMV	Cytomegalovirus	**PTT**	Partial Thromboplastin Time
EGD	Esophagogastroduodenoscopy	**DIC**	Disseminated Intravascular Coagulation
GERD	Gastroesophageal Reflux Disease	**TIBC**	Total Iron Binding Capacity
LES	Lower Esophageal Sphincter	**EDTA**	Ethylenediaminetetraacetic Acid
PPI	Proton Pump Inhibitor	**G6PD**	Glucose-6-Phophatase
HAV	Hepatitis A Virus	**RBC**	Red Blood Cell
HBV	Hepatitis B Virus	**Hgb**	Hemoglobin
IVDA	Intravenous Drug Abuse	**HbF**	Fetal Hemoglobin
HEV	Hepatitis E Virus	**HSCT**	Hematopoietic Stem Cell Transplantation
AST	Aspartate Aminotransferase	**GBM**	Glomerular Basement Membrane
ALT	Alanine Aminotransferase	**WBC**	White Blood Cell
IEA	Inferior Epigastric Artery	**ESRD**	End-Stage Renal Disease
HUS	Hemolytic Uremic Syndrome	**ABG**	Arterial Blood Gas
IV	Intravenous	**ADH**	Antidiuretic Hormone
IVF	Intravenous Fluid	**DI**	Diabetes Insipidus
CA	Carbohydrate Antigen	**CSF**	Cerebrospinal Fluid
NGT	Nasogastric Tube	**TB**	Tuberculosis

Abbreviations

AFB	Acid-Fast Bacilli
PPD	Purified Protein Derivative
VDRL	Venereal Disease Research Laboratory
RPR	Rapid Plasma Reagin
DNA	Deoxyribonucleic Acid
PIP	Proximal Interphalangeal Joints
DIP	Distal Interphalangeal Joints
PMN	Polumorphonuclear Neutrophils
AP	Anteroposterior
MTP	Metatarsophalangeal Joint
RF	Rheumatoid Factor
CK	Creatine Kinase
EMG	Electromyography
MCP	Metacarpophalangeal Joint
CCP	Cyclic Citrullinated Peptide
DMARD	Disease-Modifying Antirheumatic Drugs
HLA	Human Leukocyte Antigen
ROM	Range Of Motion
SI	Sacroiliac
TCA	Tricyclic Antidepressant
ICP	Intracranial Pressure
NMDA	N-Methyl-D-Aspartate
EEG	Electroencephalogram

TLC	Total Lung Capacity
FEV	Forced Expiratory Volume
FVC	Forced Vital Capacity
LFT	Liver Function Tests
PA	Pulmonary Arterial
PID	Pelvic Inflammatory Disease
IUD	Intrauterine Device
IVF	In Vitro Fertilization
FHR	Fetal Heart Rate
TSH	Thyroid Stimulating Hormone
FSH	Follicle Stimulating Hormone
LH	Luteinizing Hormone
OCP	Oral Contraceptive Pill
USPSTF	U.S. Preventive Services Task Force
TAH	Total Abdominal Hysterectomy
BSO	Bilateral Salpingo Oophorectomy
LMP	Last Menstrual Period
PAPP-A	Pregancy-Associated Plasma Protein A
NST	Nonstress Test
SOB	Shortness of Breath
CBT	Cognitive Behavioral Therapy

Made in the USA
San Bernardino, CA
24 February 2020